Calamity Jane

BY MARLEY RICHMOND

Kids Core
An Imprint of Abdo Publishing
abdobooks.com

abdobooks.com

Published by Abdo Publishing, a division of ABDO, PO Box 398166, Minneapolis, Minnesota 55439. Copyright © 2024 by Abdo Consulting Group, Inc. International copyrights reserved in all countries. No part of this book may be reproduced in any form without written permission from the publisher. Kids Core™ is a trademark and logo of Abdo Publishing.

Printed in the United States of America, North Mankato, Minnesota.
102023
012024

Cover Photo: German Vizulis/Shutterstock Images
Interior Photos: GL Archive/Alamy, 4–5, 28 (top); John Parrot/Stocktrek Images/Getty Images, 6; GraphicaArtis/Archive Photos/Getty Images, 8, 28 (bottom); Library of Congress/Corbis Historical/VCG/Getty Images, 10; Everett Collection/Shutterstock Images, 12–13; Red Line Editorial, 14; Shutterstock Images, 16, 29 (top); Phil Gould/Alamy, 18; Bettmann/Getty Images, 20–21, 26; IFA Film/United Archives GmbH/Alamy, 22, 29 (bottom); HBO Films/Album/Alamy, 25

Editor: Angela Lim
Series Designer: Katharine Hale

Library of Congress Control Number: 2023939616

Publisher's Cataloging-in-Publication Data

Names: Richmond, Marley, author.
Title: Calamity Jane / by Marley Richmond
Description: Minneapolis, Minnesota: Abdo Publishing, 2024 | Series: Tales from Americana | Includes online resources and index.
Identifiers: ISBN 9781098292829 (lib. bdg.) | ISBN 9798384910763 (ebook)
Subjects: LCSH: Calamity Jane, 1856-1903--Juvenile literature. | Frontier and pioneer life--Juvenile literature. | Cowgirls--Juvenile literature. | Missouri--Juvenile literature. | West United States--Juvenile literature.
Classification: DDC 398.22--dc23

CONTENTS

Calamity Jane was known for being an excellent horse rider.

A Brave Rider

A group of scouts was on a mission in the western United States. It was the early 1870s. The scouts rode on horses. A woman rode in front. She was dressed in a man's uniform. Her hair was tucked into a wide-brimmed hat.

Calamity Jane claimed to have ridden alongside General George Armstrong Custer, who fought in the Battle of Little Bighorn (1876).

The fringe on her coat and pants blew in the wind. It was clear that she was a great rider.

Suddenly, the group was attacked. They heard gunshots. It was chaos. The woman turned in her saddle to look behind her. She saw the group's leader, Captain Egan. He had been shot! He was about to fall off his horse.

She turned her horse quickly. Dust flew up behind her. She rode to his side. The woman groaned as she lifted the captain onto her saddle. They rode together to safety.

Army Scouts

The US government has a history of taking American Indian land for its own. In the late 1800s, US settlers began making homes in the West. They often forced the American Indian people who lived there to leave their homes. Some American Indians fought back against the United States. They were protecting their land. The US Army sent scouts to guard settlements from possible attacks.

Calamity Jane was known for being a good shot and wearing men's clothing.

Captain Egan recovered. He gave the woman a nickname. He called her Calamity Jane. He said she was a **heroine** of the plains.

Fact or Fiction?

Calamity Jane's real name was Martha Canary. Canary became a larger-than-life figure. Calamity Jane was famous in the United States. People thought she didn't act the way a woman was supposed to at that time. She was an excellent rider and had great aim with a gun.

Canary told many stories about her life. But historians think that many of these stories are untrue. She claimed that she and Captain Egan were on a mission for General George Armstrong Custer when she got her nickname.

Though Martha Canary was a real person, many stories about Calamity Jane are untrue.

But there is no record that she rode with either man. This is one of the many **legends** about Calamity Jane.

Canary wrote about her time as a scout in her **autobiography**. She wrote:

> As a scout, I had a great many dangerous missions to perform, and . . . [I] always succeeded in getting away safely. . . . I was considered the most . . . daring rider and one of the best shots in the western country.

Source: Martha Canary. "The Autobiography of Calamity Jane." *Project Gutenberg Australia*, n.d., gutenberg.net.au. Accessed 14 Apr. 2023.

What's the Big Idea?

Read this quote carefully. What is its main idea? Explain how the main idea is supported by details.

In the mid-1800s, more than 300,000 people moved to the western United States.

CHAPTER 2

Martha Canary

Martha Canary was born in Princeton, Missouri, in the 1850s. Her family moved to Montana when she was a child. They traveled in a wagon for many months to get there.

Canary said she learned how to shoot and hunt on this journey.

Calamity Jane's Journey West

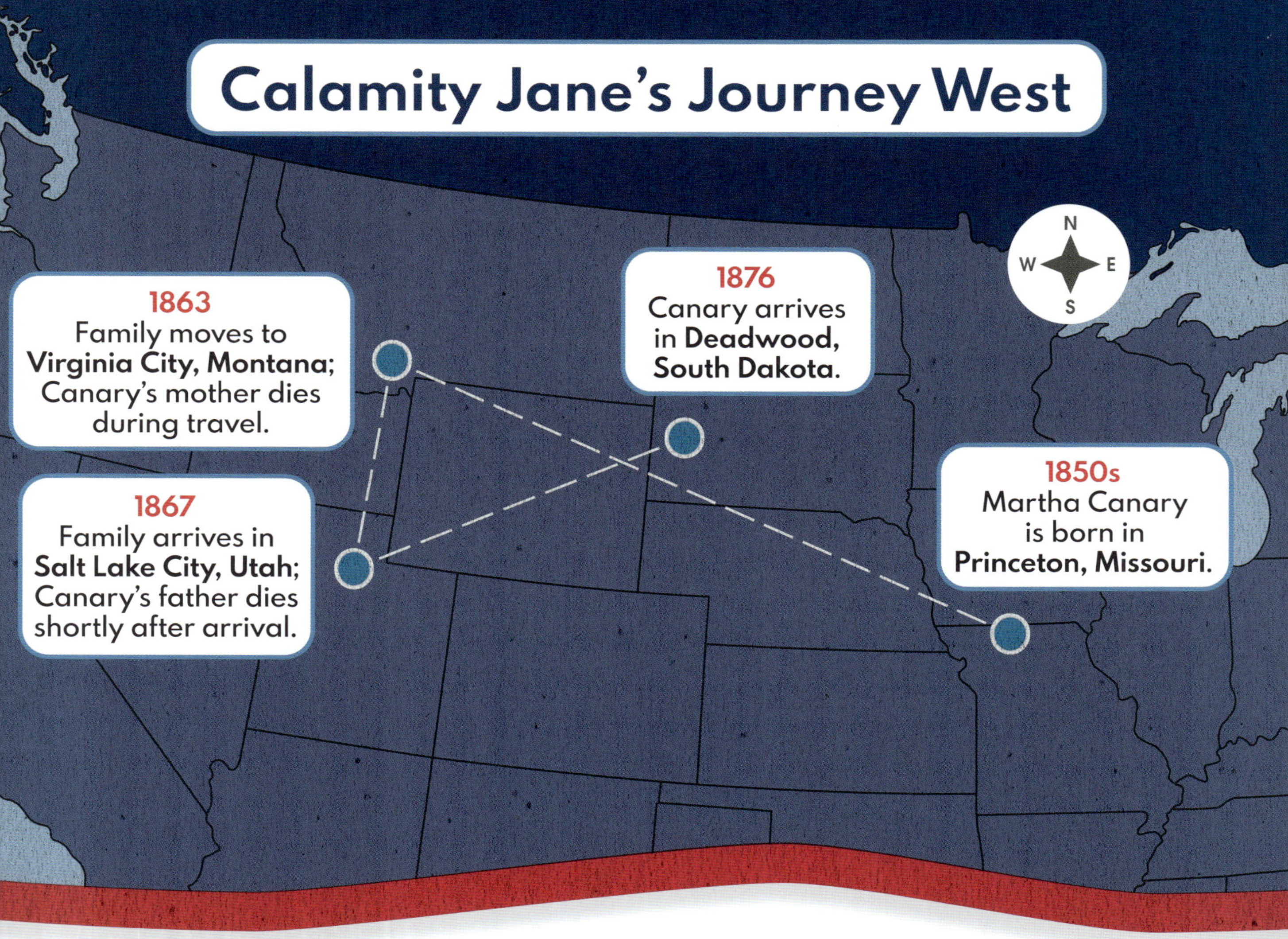

Martha Canary was born in Missouri. Her family traveled west in the 1860s before Canary found herself in Deadwood in 1876.

She became a fearless rider and crossed dangerous rivers with her horse. She claimed they escaped death many times. However, these stories were **exaggerated**.

Canary's mother died on the trip to Montana. Her father died a few years later, when Canary was about 12 years old. She was the oldest of her siblings. She had to take care of them. She took any job she could to make money.

Becoming Calamity Jane

Not much is known about Canary's teenage years. Canary claims that she was a scout in the early 1870s. She says this was when the nickname Calamity Jane took hold.

In 1876, Canary moved to Deadwood, South Dakota. By that time, her nickname was well known. In Deadwood, Calamity Jane became more famous. She got to Deadwood at the same time as Wild Bill Hickok.

Today, Deadwood still celebrates its connection to famous legends such as Wild Bill Hickok.

He was another legend of the West. Many stories are told about the pair. Some stories say they were secretly married. But there is no evidence that they were. Hickok was already married when he met Calamity Jane. He knew her for only a few weeks. Hickok was killed shortly after arriving in Deadwood.

Calamity Jane was known for having a fiery **temper**. Stories say she was quick to get angry. She could be violent. But there was a gentler side of Calamity Jane too. There was a smallpox **epidemic** in 1878. Many people stayed away from others so they would not get sick.

Wild West Shows

In 1895, Calamity Jane joined a Wild West show. These performances were popular at the time. Many were like a circus or a rodeo. Calamity Jane showed off her shooting skills as a performer.

Martha Canary married a man named Clinton Burke in 1891. She was then sometimes known as Martha Burke. Tourists can visit her grave and that of Wild Bill Hickok in Deadwood.

But Calamity Jane cared for sick people without worrying about her own health.

In 1896, Calamity Jane published her **autobiography**. It was a collection of tall tales.

The autobiography added to Calamity Jane's fame. It shaped many of the legends told about her today.

Martha Canary died in 1903. She was buried next to Wild Bill Hickok. Some Deadwood locals said the town was playing a joke on Hickok. They thought Hickok hadn't liked Canary when they were alive. They claimed she would annoy him in the afterlife.

Further Evidence

Look at the website below. Does it give any new evidence to support Chapter Two?

Calamity Jane

abdocorelibrary.com/calamity-jane

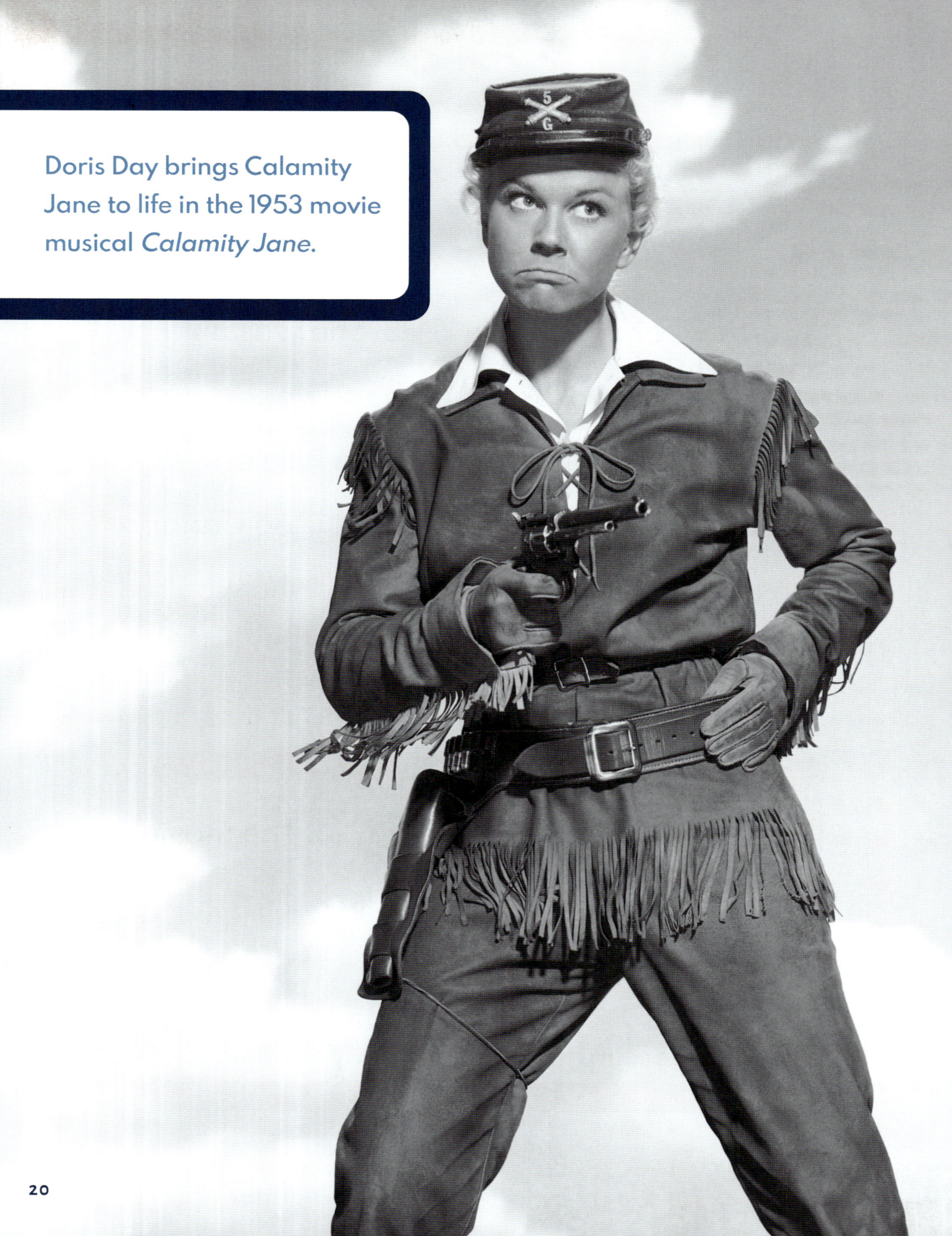

Doris Day brings Calamity Jane to life in the 1953 movie musical *Calamity Jane.*

CHAPTER 3

On the Big Screen

The legend of Calamity Jane lived on after Canary's death. In 1953, the movie musical *Calamity Jane* was released. The movie follows her life in Deadwood. In the movie, Calamity Jane's outfit includes a brown jacket, cowboy boots, and pants.

The 1953 movie explored Calamity Jane's relationship with Wild Bill Hickok.

During Canary's lifetime, pants were considered men's clothing. Most legends about Calamity Jane say she wore men's clothes all the time. But in reality, historians say Martha Canary also wore dresses.

During her life, Canary said she was a Pony Express rider. Riders in the Pony Express delivered mail. Canary said she always rode the most dangerous route. These stories inspired a scene in the 1953 movie. Calamity Jane rides a **stagecoach** to bring packages to Deadwood.

The Pony Express

Pony Express riders carried mail on horseback between Missouri and California. The official Pony Express lasted only from 1860 to 1861. A story about Calamity Jane says she was a rider in 1876. Canary may have delivered mail, but she probably wasn't part of the Pony Express.

She travels through a dangerous area where people might try to steal them. Calamity Jane protects the stagecoach.

In the movie, Calamity Jane is given a more traditional love story than the real Martha Canary ever had. The movie ends with Wild Bill Hickok marrying Calamity Jane. This scene reflected popular tales about their relationship before Wild Bill Hickok's death.

Calamity Jane on TV

In the early 2000s, HBO released a series called *Deadwood*. The show was for mature audiences. On the show, the character of Calamity Jane was rough and tough.

Robin Weigert plays Calamity Jane in the *Deadwood* television series.

In *Deadwood*, Calamity Jane is known for her temper. But she also shows kindness. She helps care for a child whose parents were killed.

She also nurses sick and injured people back to health.

Legends about Calamity Jane show many of the traits that people valued during Canary's lifetime. Calamity Jane represents the toughness and independence needed to survive in the West. She showed that women could be strong and kind at the same time.

William Elsey Connelley wrote a book about Calamity Jane. He described her time in Deadwood, helping people with smallpox:

> Out of her own small resources, she took money for food and medicines for those too poor to buy their own . . . going constantly . . . on her errands of kindness.

Source: James D. McLaird. *Calamity Jane.* University of Oklahoma Press, 2005, p. 229.

Comparing Texts

Think about the quote. Does it support the information in this chapter? Or does it give a different perspective? Explain how in a few sentences.

Legendary Facts

Calamity Jane's real name was Martha Canary. There are many stories about how she got her famous nickname.

Calamity Jane was known for being a good shot.

Calamity Jane spent much of her life in Deadwood, South Dakota, which was also home to Wild Bill Hickok.

Calamity Jane was a musical released in 1953. It tells a romantic story of Calamity Jane's time in Deadwood.

Glossary

autobiography
a nonfiction history written about the author's life from his or her personal memories or experiences

epidemic
an outbreak of a disease that spreads quickly

exaggerated
became more dramatic or larger than life

heroine
a female hero

legend
a famous story of the past that is not always true

stagecoach
a large carriage pulled by horses that travels along an established route

temper
an ability to get irritated or angry

Online Resources

To learn more about Calamity Jane, visit our free resource websites below.

Visit **abdocorelibrary.com** or scan this QR code for free Common Core resources for teachers and students, including vetted activities, multimedia, and booklinks, for deeper subject comprehension.

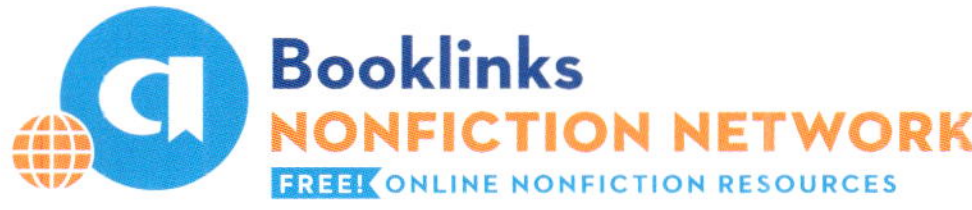

Visit **abdobooklinks.com** or scan this QR code for free additional online weblinks for further learning. These links are routinely monitored and updated to provide the most current information available.

Learn More

Lowe, Mifflin. *The True West*. Bushel and Peck, 2020.

Richmond, Marley. *Pecos Bill*. Abdo, 2024.

Tieck, Sarah. *South Dakota*. Abdo, 2020.

Index

About the Author

Marley Richmond is a children's book editor and author. She lives in Minnesota with her cat, Bean.